My Catholic Saints Activity Book

Reproducible Sheets for Home and School

Written and Illustrated by Jennifer Galvin

Ambassador Children's Books
New York/Mahwah, NJ

For The Stone Soup Sisters, a saintly group of women who keep me on track through thick and thin.

Cover design by Jennifer Conlan
Cover illustration by Jennifer Galvin

ISBN: 978-0-8091-6750-0

Published by Ambassador Books
An imprint of Paulist Press
997 Macarthur Boulevard
Mahwah, New Jersey 07430

www.ambassadorbooks.com

Printed and bound in the United States of America
by Versa Press, Peoria, IL
January 2010

The Saints

Saints are people whose extraordinary lives and devotion to God have been officially recognized by the Church. Saints are canonized by the Pope.

A patron saint is a saint to whose protection and intercession a person, a society, or a place is dedicated. Many countries have patron saints. There are also patron saints for crafts and trades and other activities. Catholic Churches have patron saints.

In our prayers, we can ask saints to intercede to God for us. For instance, we might ask St. Thomas Aquinas, the patron saint of schools, to intercede on our behalf when we need help with studies or a test.

All Saints Day is celebrated on November 1 for all of the people who knew Christ while on this earth but are now in heaven with God.

Solemnity of Mary

The Blessed Virgin Mary is the Mother of God. She is the patron saint of the United States and many other countries. We celebrate the Solemnity of Mary on January 1. Color this picture of Mary and Jesus. Remember that we can ask Mary for help when we need it.

St. Thomas Aquinas

St. Thomas Aquinas is the patron saint of schools and students. We celebrate his feast on January 28. Match the school supplies to their shadows. Then color the school supplies.

St. Blase

We celebrate St. Blase's feast on February 3. He is the patron saint of sore throats and veterinarians. Priests bless our throats on St. Blase Day with what you will find when you finish this dot-to-dot. Complete the dot-to-dot, then fill in the blanks and color the picture you have created.

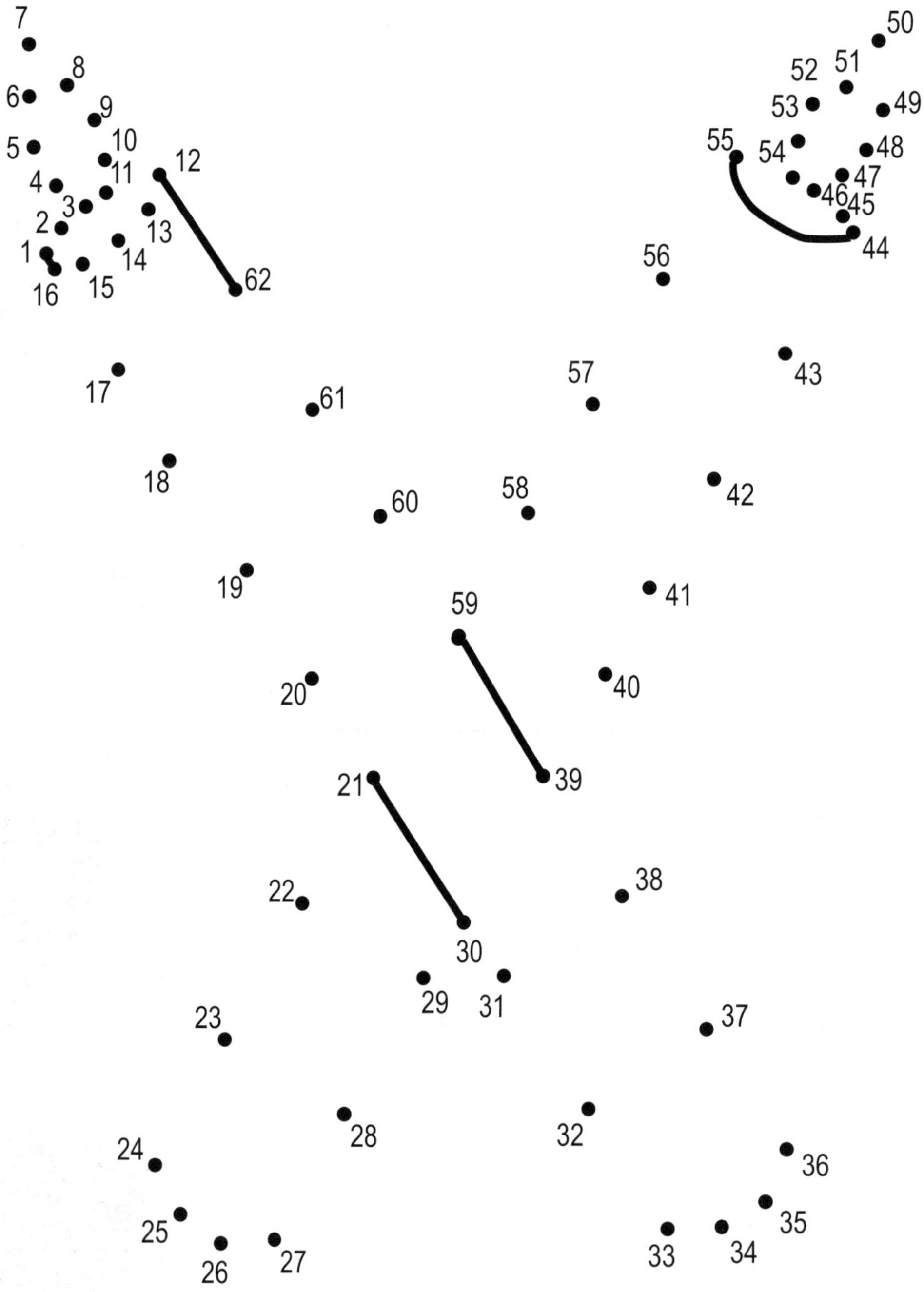

Priests bless a person's throat with two _ _ _ _ _ _ _.

St. Agatha

St. Agatha is the patron saint of nurses, fire fighters, and for protection against earthquakes. We celebrate her feast on February 5. Find and circle all twelve things that are different in the second picture. Then color the pictures.

February 6

Whose feast do we celebrate on February 6? He was a Japanese Jesuit preacher who was martyred along with 25 others for his faith. He also had the right to dress as a Samurai. To find out who this saint is, crack the code and fill in the blanks below.

A: 5+2= __	B: 1+1= __	C: 9+8= __	D: 10+3= __
E: 7+3= __	F: 8+8= __	G: 11+11= __	H: 25+1= __
I: 6+2= __	J: 3+2= __	K: 3+1= __	L: 2+1= __
M: 8+3= __	N: 9+9= __	O: 11+8= __	P: 6+3= __
Q: 22+2= __	R: 10+13= __	S: 5+1= __	T: 10+11= __
U: 9+6= __	V: 6+6= __	W: 8+6= __	X: 1+0= __
Y: 12+13= __	Z: 10+10= __		

___ ___   ___ ___ ___ ___   ___ ___ ___ ___

6 21   9 7 15 3   11 8 4 8

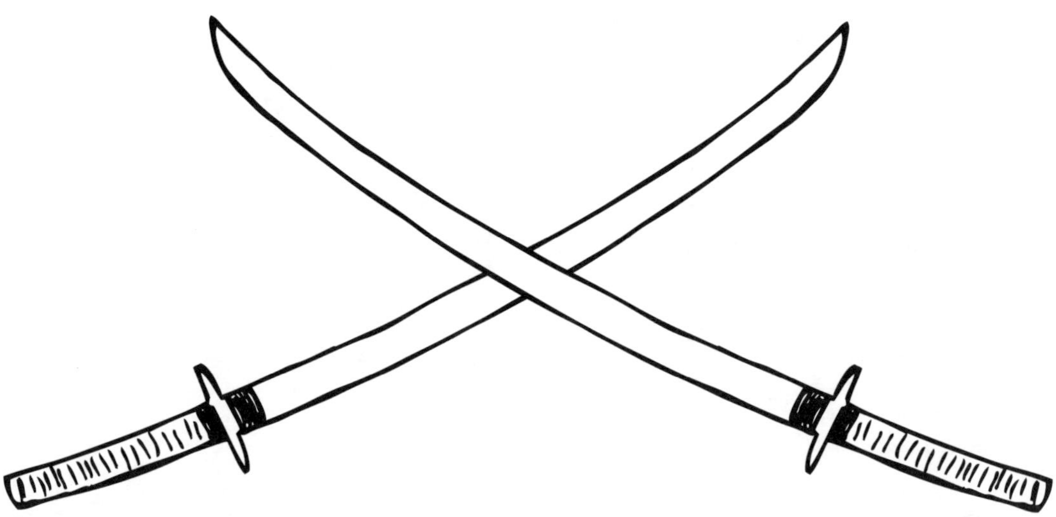

St. Patrick

St. Patrick is the patron saint of Ireland. We celebrate his feast on March 17. He brought the Catholic faith to the Irish people. Tradition claims that St. Patrick drove all the snakes out of Ireland. Color by number to find a special symbol that St. Patrick used to teach people about God, Jesus, and the Holy Spirit. What is hiding behind the symbol?

1= Brown 2= Green 3= Blue 4= Purple

St. Joseph

St. Joseph is Jesus' father. He was a carpenter. He is the patron saint of carpenters and families. We celebrate his feast on March 19. Complete the dot-to-dot to see some of the tools that St. Joseph would have used as a carpenter. After you finish the dot-to-dot, fill in the blanks below.

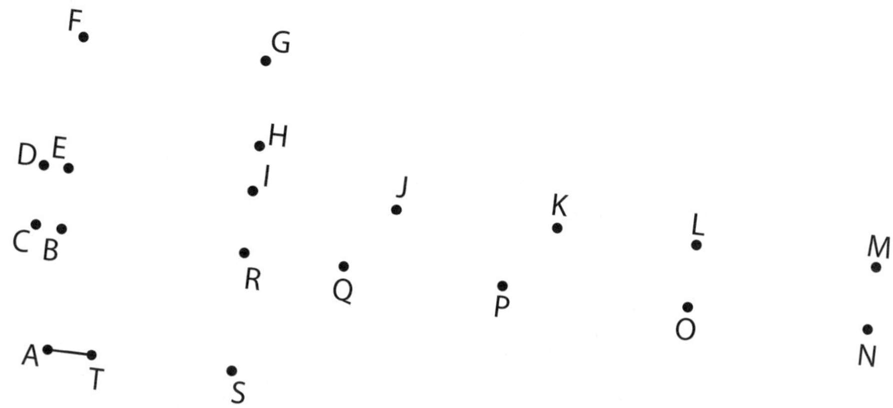

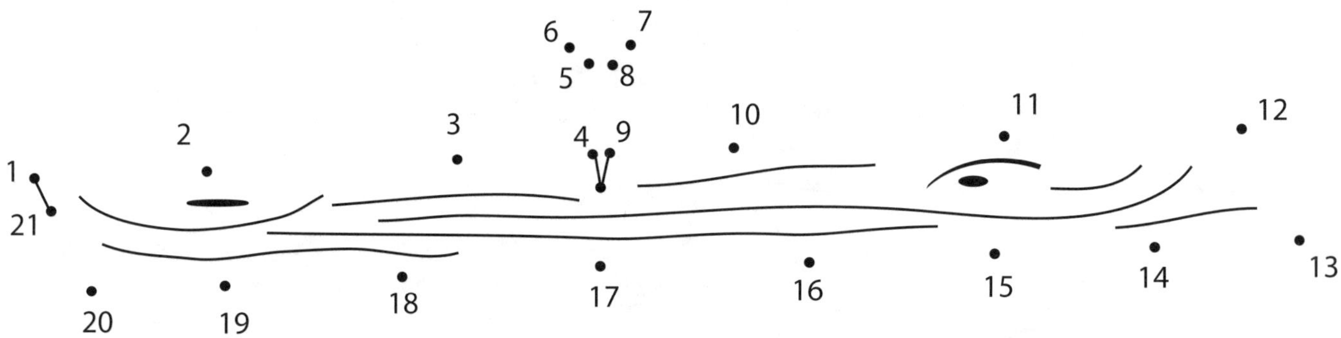

Some of the things that Joseph used in his carpentry work were _ _ _ _ _ _, _ _ _ _, and a _ _ _ _ _ _ _.

St. George

We celebrate St. George's feast on April 23. He is the patron saint of England and soldiers. Color by number to see what tradition says that St. George is famous for slaying. Then fill in the answer in the blanks below.

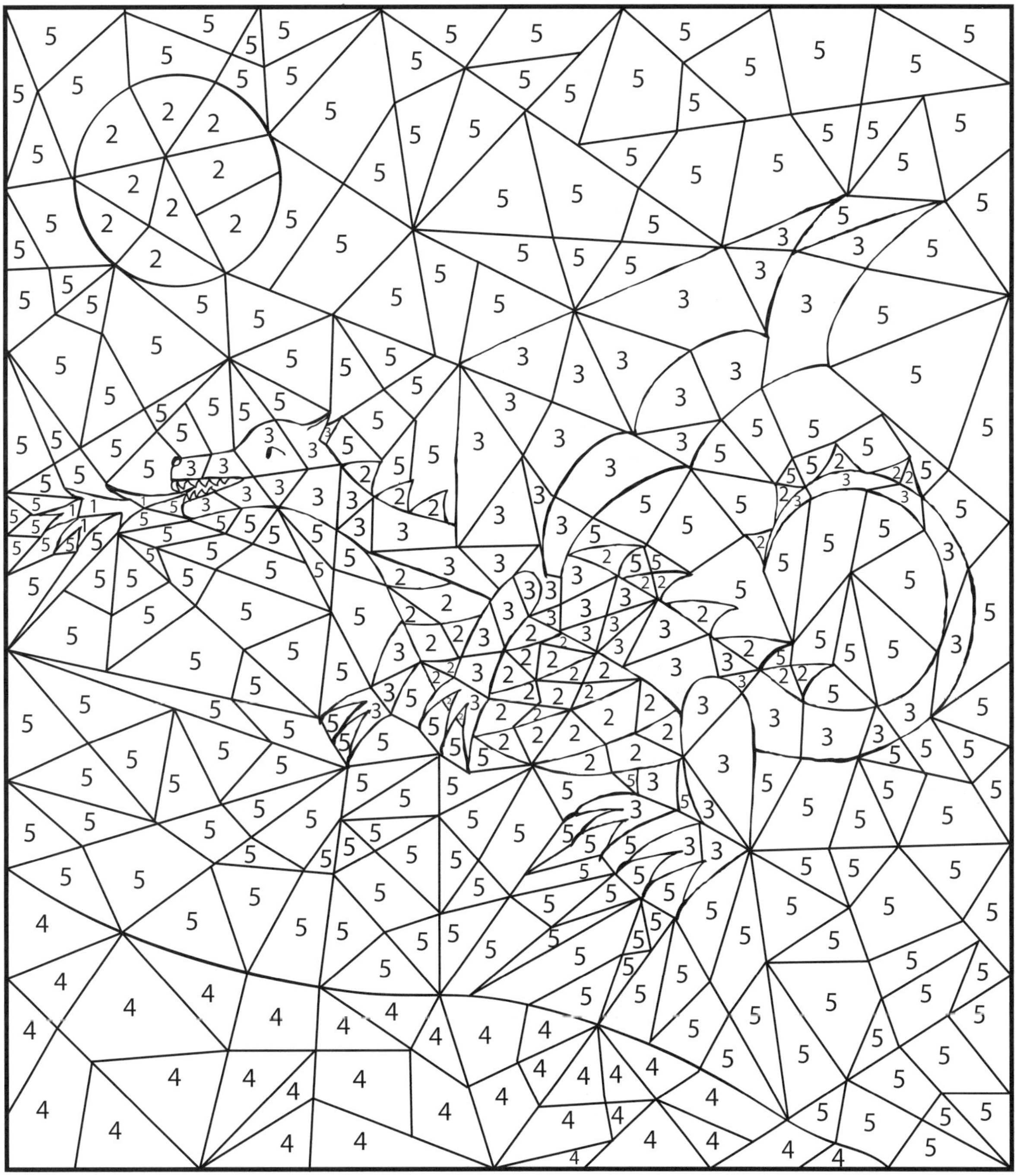

1=orange 2=yellow 3=red 4=green 5=blue

St. George slew a _ _ _ _ _ _.

St. Joan of Arc

We celebrate St. Joan of Arc's feast on May 30. She is the patron saint of soldiers and one of the patron saints of France. She believed God sent her voices of saints and angels to help her save France. She led France into battle many times. How many swords can you count?

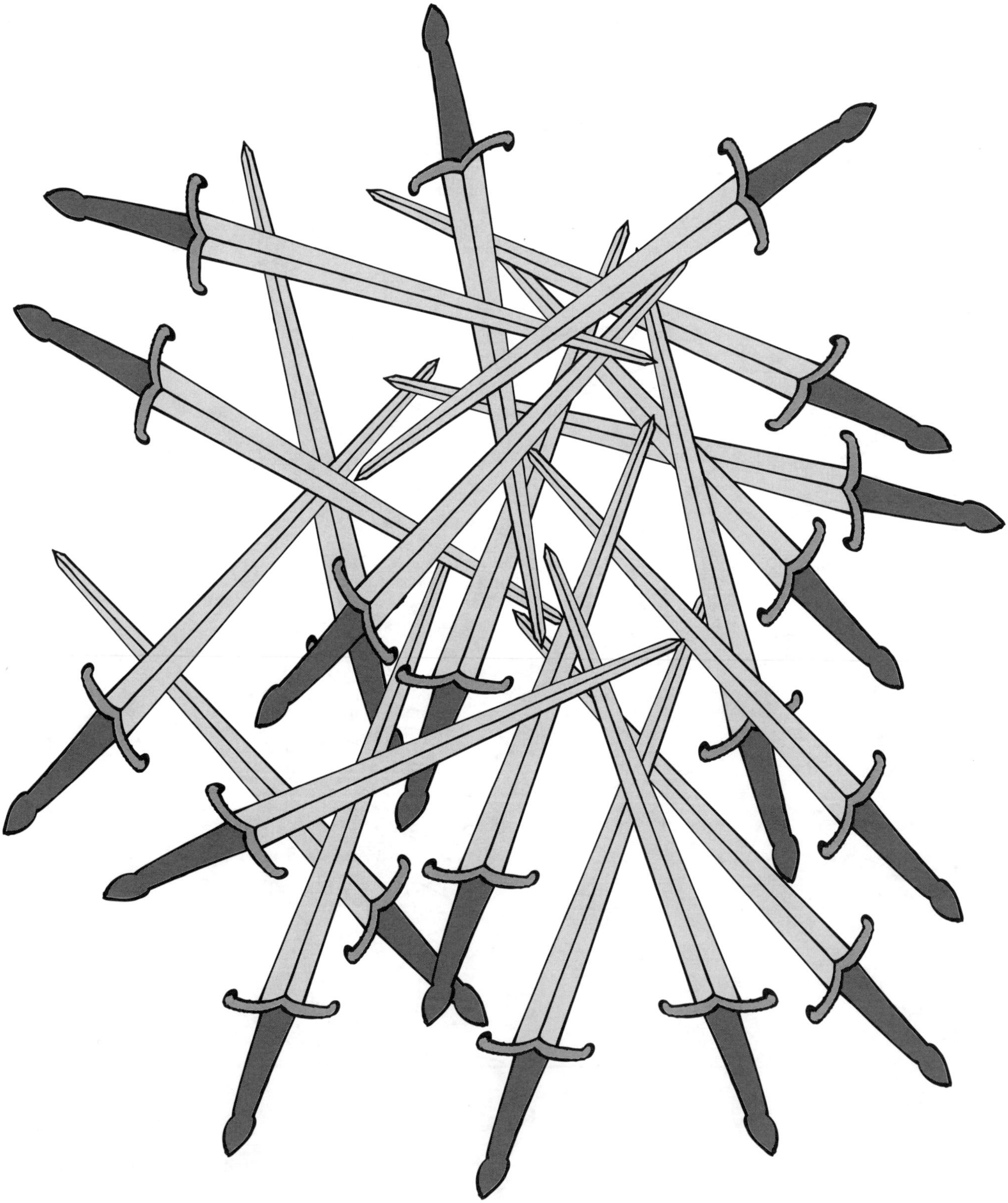

St. Erasmus (Elmo)

We celebrate the feast of St. Elmo, the patron saint of sailors, on June 2. Sometimes during thunderstorms, sailors saw "Saint Elmo's Fire" (an electrical charge that resembles lightning) on the masts of their ships. They believed it was a sign that the storm was about to end. Circle the ten things that are different in the second picture.

St. Anthony of Padua

St. Anthony of Padua's feast day is celebrated on June 13. He is the patron saint associated with helping us find lost items. Find the twelve things hidden in this picture. Circle them and then color the picture.

St. Peter

St. Peter is the patron saint of fishermen. He was the very first Pope and is known for holding the keys to heaven. We celebrate his feast day jointly with St. Paul on June 29. Color by number.

1=red 2=yellow 3=purple 4=grey
5=green 6=light blue 7=dark blue 8=white

St. Martha

We celebrate St. Martha's feast day on July 29. Trace the lines from the boxes to the letters. Then fill in the boxes with the letters to find out what group honors St. Martha as their patron saint.

St. Martha is the patron saint of:

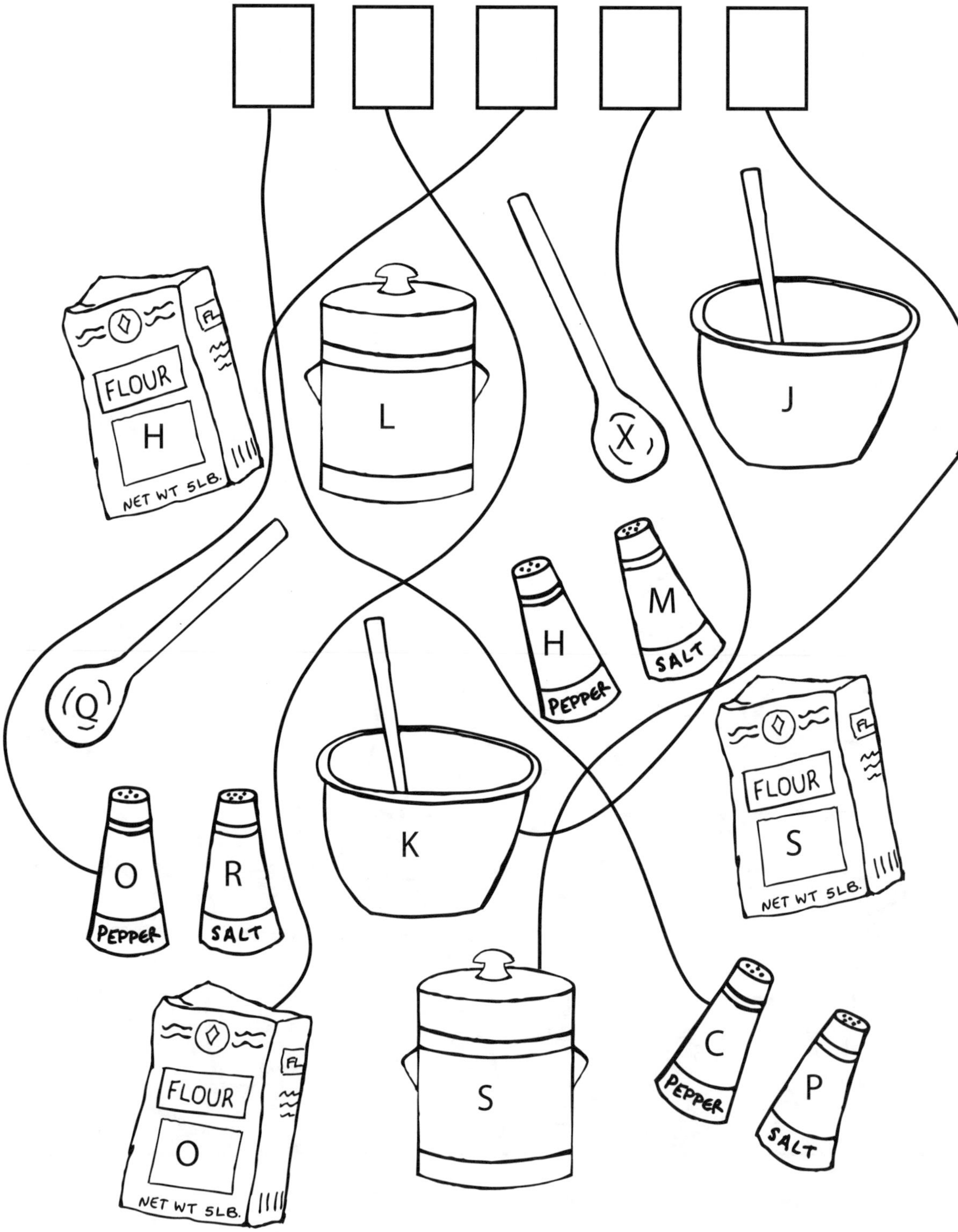

St. Clare of Assisi

St. Clare of Assisi is the patron saint of embroiderers, television, and good weather. Her feast day is celebrated on August 11. Circle the eleven things that are wrong with this picture. Then color the picture.

St. Moses the Black

We celebrate the feast of St. Moses the Black on August 28. He is the patron saint of Africa. Follow the maze to help St. Moses the Black get to his sand and then back to the monastery.

St. Gregory the Great

St. Gregory the Great is the patron saint of singers. We celebrate his feast on September 3. Connect the dots to find a musical surprise!

St. Vincent de Paul

We celebrate St. Vincent de Paul's feast day on September 27. St. Vincent de Paul is the patron saint of works of charity. Match these children with the works of charity they are about to do. Then color the children and their charity work.

St. Gabriel, St. Michael, and St. Raphael

St. Gabriel, St. Michael, and St. Raphael are archangels. We celebrate their feast on September 29. St. Gabriel is the patron saint of messengers. St. Michael is the patron saint of soldiers and the sick. St. Raphael is the patron saint of doctors and travelers. Color their picture.

St. Thérèse

St. Thérèse is a patron saint of France and the missions. We celebrate her feast on October 1. Color by number to find the popular name that St. Thérèse is known by, then fill in the blanks below.

1=red 2=yellow 3=purple 4=blue 5=green

St. Thérèse was also known as "The Little _ _ _ _ _ _."

St. Francis of Assisi

St. Francis of Assisi's feast is celebrated on October 4. He is the patron saint of Italy and animals. See if you can find the twelve objects hidden in this picture. Circle them and then color the picture.

St. Luke

St. Luke is the patron saint of doctors and artists. We celebrate his feast on October 18. Circle the two items that are exactly the same.

October 28

Which saint's feast do we celebrate on October 28? He is the patron saint of those in deepest trouble. Crack the code to find out. Fill in the blanks at the bottom of the page with the letter that matches the number under the blank.

A: 6-5= ___	H: 14-2= ___	O: 26-1= ___	U: 10-2= ___
B: 7-2= ___	I: 8-4= ___	P: 20-9= ___	V: 26-13= ___
C: 27-1= ___	J: 26-3= ___	Q: 23-4= ___	W: 16-2= ___
D: 19-2= ___	K: 13-3= ___	R: 26-2= ___	X: 26-5= ___
E: 10-1= ___	L: 25-3= ___	S: 8-1= ___	Y: 19-3= ___
F: 22-2= ___	M: 8-2= ___	T: 6-3= ___	Z: 19-4= ___
G: 20-2= ___	N: 6-4= ___		

___ ___   ___ ___ ___ ___

7 3   23 8 17 9

All Saints Day

All Saints Day is celebrated on November 1. This is the day when we celebrate all the saints who are now with Christ in heaven. When we go to mass on All Saints Day, we might see some of the things in this picture.

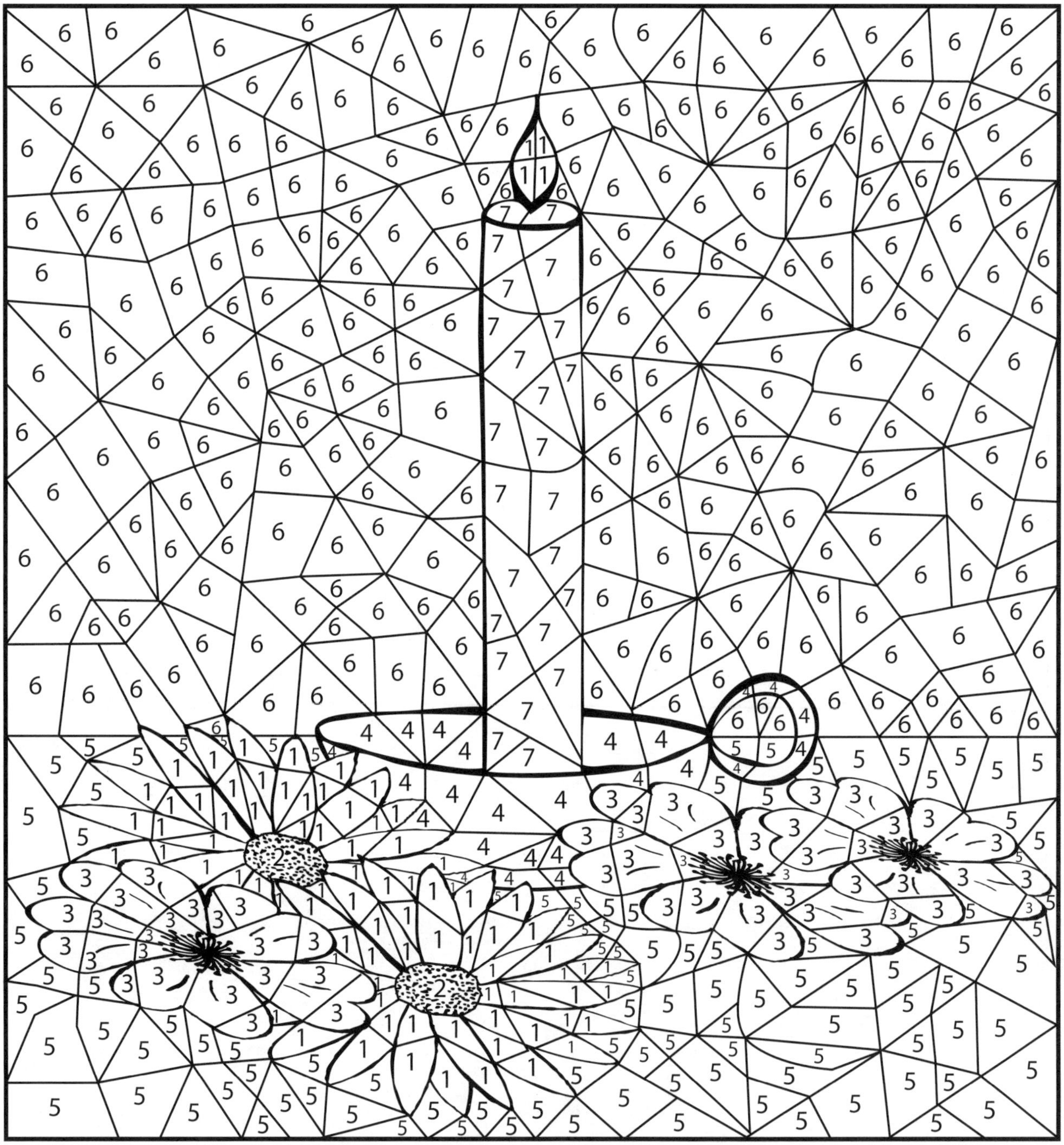

1=yellow 2=red 3=purple 4=gray
5=brown 6=blue 7=white

St. Martin de Porres

St. Martin de Porres is the patron saint of social justice. His feast is celebrated on November 3. St. Martin de Porres saved the mice at his monastery by telling the mice that if they would just go outside, he would feed them every day. Match each set of mice to their shadows.

St. Andrew

St. Andrew is the patron saint of fishermen. St. Andrew was one of Jesus' disciples. We celebrate his feast on November 30. How many fish do you count?

St. Juan Diego

The Virgin Mary appeared to St. Juan Diego and an image of her impressed on his cloak. He built a church in her honor on the spot that his miracle occurred. Help St. Juan Diego go through the maze to Our Lady of Guadalupe.

Trace the Line

This saint is the patron saint of friendship and writers. His feast is celebrated on December 27. To find out who this saint is, trace the lines from the boxes to the letters, and then fill in a letter in each of the boxes.

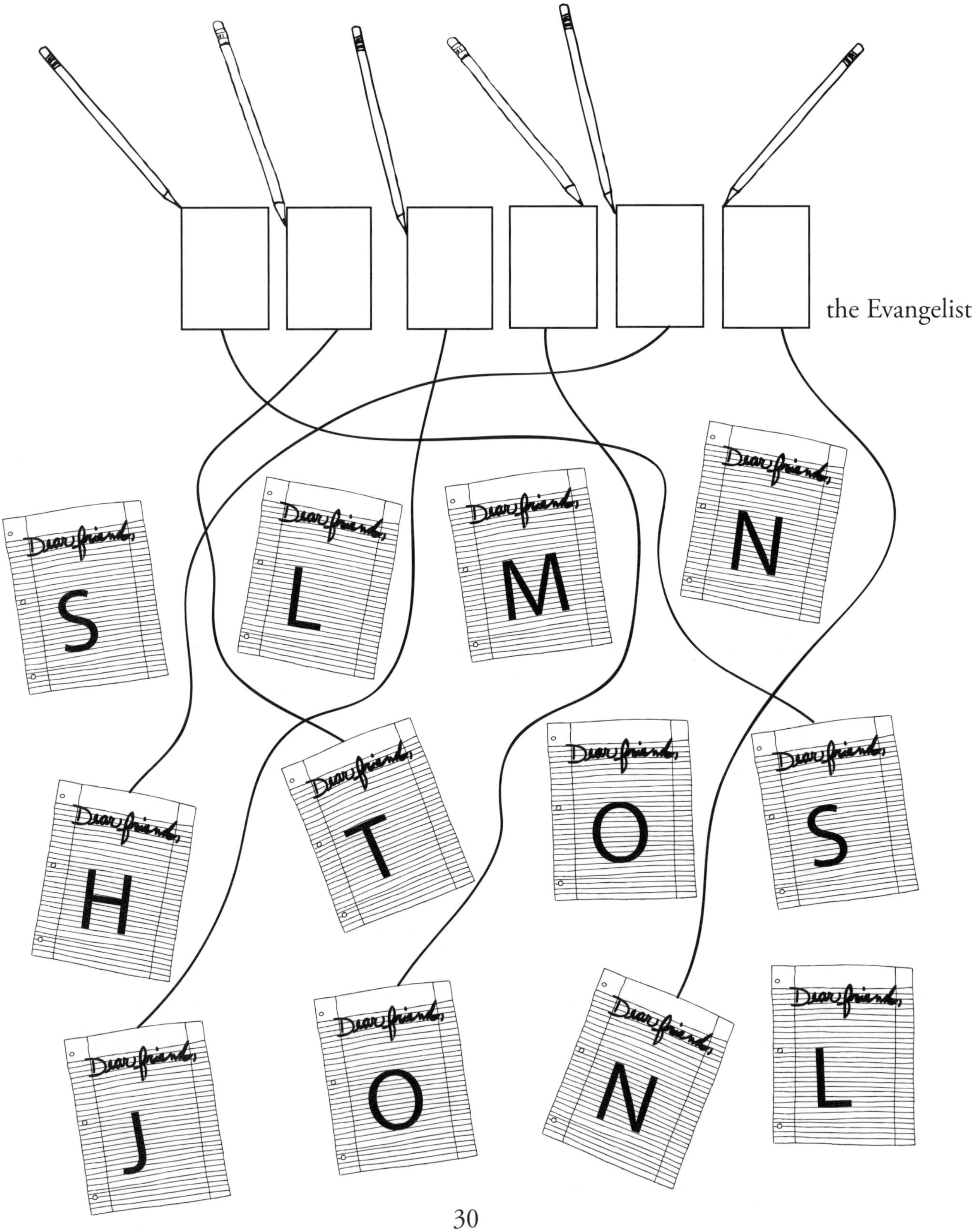

Answers

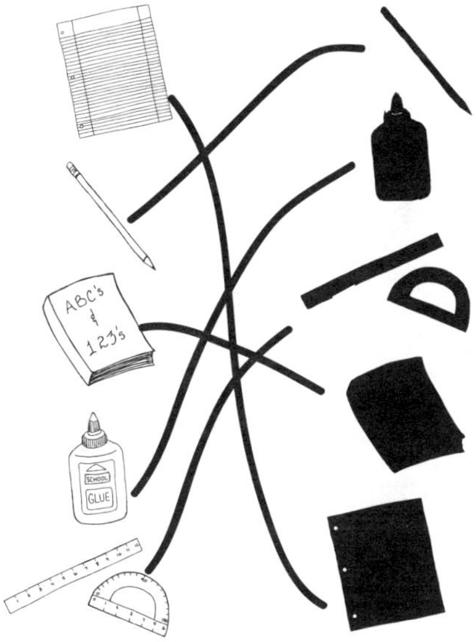

Page 5

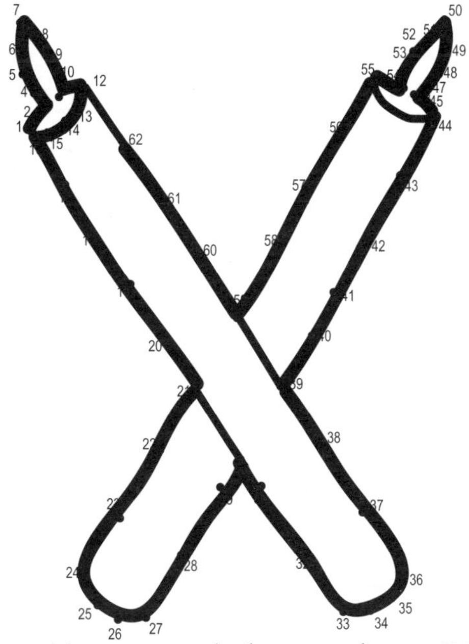

Priests bless a person's throat with two CANDLES.
Page 6

Page 14

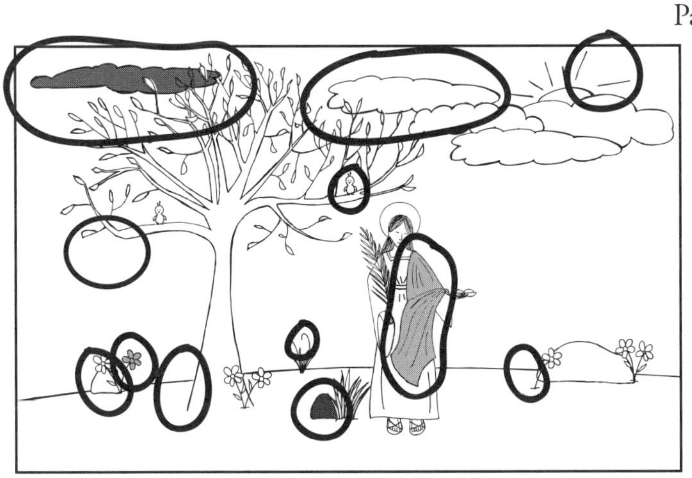

Page 7

A: 5+2= 7	B: 1+1= 2	C: 9+8= 17	D: 10+3= 13
E: 7+3= 10	F: 8+8= 16	G: 11+11= 22	H: 25+1= 26
I: 6+2= 8	J: 3+2= 5	K: 3+1= 4	L: 2+1= 3
M: 8+3= 11	N: 9+9= 18	O: 11+8= 19	P: 6+3= 9
Q: 22+2= 24	R: 10+13= 23	S: 5+1= 6	T: 10+11= 21
U: 9+6= 15	V: 6+6= 12	W: 8+6= 14	X: 1+0= 1
Y: 12+13= 25	Z: 10+10= 20		

S T   P A U L   M I K I
6 21   9 7 15 3   11 8 4 8

Page 8

A snake is hiding behind the shamrock.
Page 9

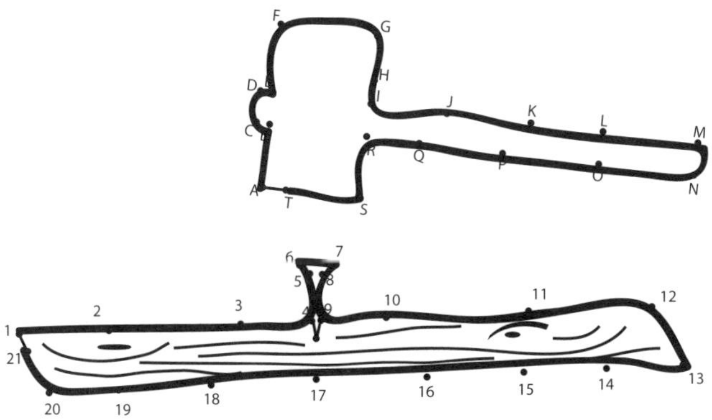

NAILS, WOOD, and a HAMMER.
Page 10

Page 13

St. George slew a dragon.
Page 11

COOKS
Page 16

There are 20 swords.
Page 12

Answers

Page 17

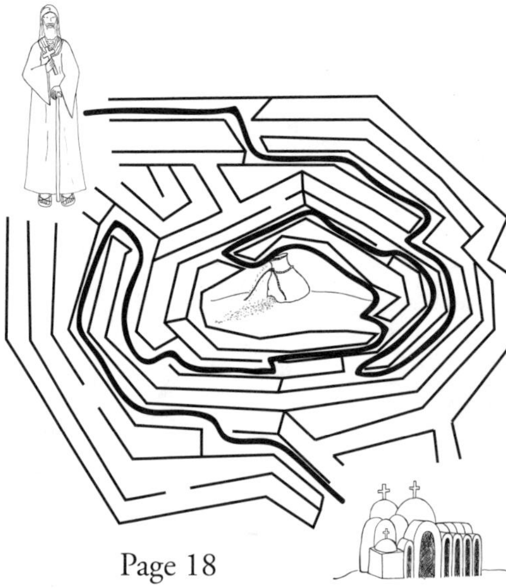

Page 18

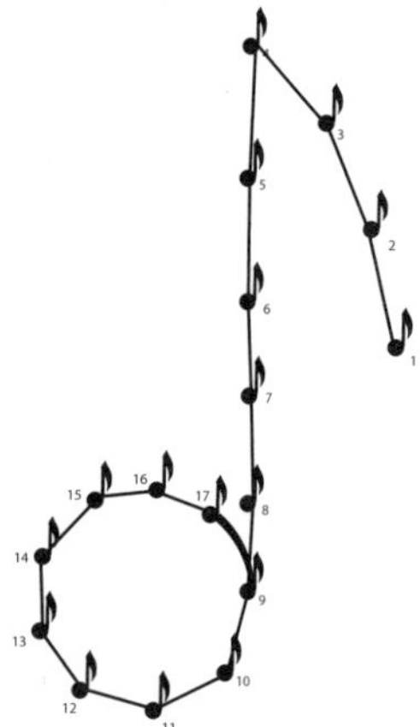

Page 19

St. Therese was also known as The Little FLOWER.
Page 22

Page 20

Page 23

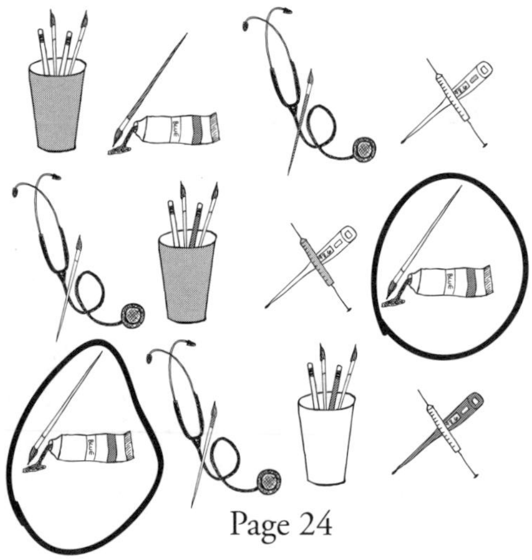

Page 24

Page 27

A: 6-5= 1	H: 14-2= 2	O: 26-1=25	U: 10-2= 8
B: 7-2= 5	I: 8-4= 4	P: 20-9= 11	V: 26-13= 13
C: 27-1= 26	J: 26-3= 23	Q: 23-4= 19	W: 16-2= 14
D: 19-2= 17	K: 13-3= 10	R: 26-2= 24	X: 26-5= 21
E: 10-1= 9	L: 25-3= 22	S: 8-1= 7	Y: 19-3= 16
F: 22-2= 20	M: 8-2= 6	T: 6-3= 3	Z: 19-4= 15
G: 20-2= 18	N: 6-4= 2		

S	T		J	U	D	E
7	3		23	8	17	9

Page 25

Page 29

There are 36 fish.
Page 28

ST JOHN the Evangelist
Page 30